CHANGE IS A CHOICE

CHANGE IS A CHOICE

EARNIE LARSEN
with Carol Larsen Hegarty

Wisdom from *Old Patterns, New Truths* and *Days of Healing, Days of Joy*

Hazelden Educational Materials
Center City, Minnesota 55012-0176

ISBN: 0-89486-897-7

EDITOR'S NOTE

Hazelden Educational Materials offers a variety of information on chemical dependency and related areas. Our publications do not necessarily represent Hazelden's programs, nor do they officially speak for any Twelve Step organization.

CHANGE
IS A CHOICE

I formed my habits, and my habits formed my future.
—*J.T.*

Change implies a vital truth for all of us: We have a choice. There is a way out of the trap of our old patterns. Many of us have unwittingly perpetuated fear, self-delusion, perfectionism, and resentments in our relationships and daily interactions. Some of us even think crisis follows us like a shadow. The fact is, some of us drag that shadow around with us. We can release that shadow of past burdens and see ourselves in a new light—if we're willing to first look at the ways we've been acting out our old behaviors.

Many of us are masters at giving away our power. We are often ego-driven, outer-directed people. As such, we base our lives on the values and decisions of others; this includes what we should or should not do, what we can and cannot do, and what we must or must not do. We don't act on our personal values. We react rather than act.

Even those of us who are volatile and short-fused, boasting "No one's going to tell me what to do," are giving away our power. We're allowing others to dictate how we respond to situations. By always doing the opposite of what we feel someone is telling us, we are emotionally handcuffed. We are not acting. We are reacting to what we perceive is directed at us, and those perceptions are based on yesterday's experiences. Who we are reacting to may not be the person in front of us, but someone from the past, long gone or long dead.

Whenever we allow others to assume our decision-making ability, we sacrifice our integrity by giving away our power. And the result is stress. In the upcoming pages, I'll discuss how this stress actually feeds into a cycle that we've unwittingly set up for ourselves, a cycle that gathers momentum and grows as we continue to act out our old patterns. Once we begin to identify these patterns, we'll see how they contribute to this cycle and we'll learn how to stop this from happening.

Once the patterns are clear and we understand the ways we've allowed the patterns to cause chaos in our lives, we can then be responsible for healthier behaviors.

When we start making positive changes, we restore our integrity by discovering that we have choices and by experiencing success—however subtle or profound. As we begin practicing healthier behaviors, we find that hope and serenity have become a part of our lives. As our choices yield positive results, we are reinforced in our desire to achieve and maintain this process.

Yes, we have been affected by our pasts, but we don't have to remain victims as a result. While we may have had terrible experiences, the course of our future is up to us. By breaking the cycle that was set in motion so long ago by our parents, and perhaps grandparents, we can model a better life for our children.

It's one thing to find freedom to talk about anger, rage, and pain. It's quite another to identify the lurking patterns that were learned and integrated into our personalities as a result of these traumatic episodes. Our capacity to genuinely alter these patterns lies at the very heart of the process of change. And the first step in this process is to understand these patterns.

Practice makes perfect.

Whether it's playing the piano or making mountains out of molehills, if we practice it long enough, we get good at it. That's what habits are—proficiencies born of practice. Habits may be conscious or unconscious, healthy or unhealthy, attractive or repulsive, important or trivial.

Our habits form our future. Just as a train is directed by the rails it runs along, our lives are directed by our habits. Unless we build new rails, new habits, our lives will continue to move through the same old places on the same old rails. How could it be any other way?

Habits are powerful—mostly because they're too deep to be visible. But they're there and operating all the time. We need to be aware of what our habits are. Every confrontation with an unfriendly habit is a singular victory. Every time we lay a new foot of track in a different direction we affect the quality of our future. Every time counts.

The Consequences of Old Patterns

Again, it is one thing to vent outrage and sadness over past trauma. It is quite another matter to see clearly that the present painful consequences are the result of continuing to act out these past patterns.

The more the origins of these painful present

consequences remain shrouded in mystery and confusion the less power we have to deal with them. We need to understand where we hurt today, why we hurt today, how we get into the situations that cause hurt today, and how we continue to create the very situations we despised in the past.

But if we are to change, if we are to overcome the obstacles to happiness and a freer life, we must understand what the underlying bases are. The first step in untying a knot is to know where it is and what kind of a knot it is.

Healing Is the Goal

Yes, there may have been appalling crimes committed against us in the past, but the torch has now been passed to us. It is now our responsibility to identify the damage clearly, take responsibility, and act appropriately to climb up and out.

Change requires new behaviors, in addition to exploring thoughts and feelings. The behavior required for change is not easy and is often downright painful. If it were not so, change would be an easy drive.

Rita grew up with what she now calls "snob-itis." However, although her family believed it was "better than the rest," she never was. Rita lived under the constant admonition: "What will the neighbors say?" Even though she was expected to produce and live up to certain standards, she never felt cared about.

Rita came to believe that wanting the warmth that she later called intimacy was a trap. For her, intimacy led to vulnerability, which led to taking a risk, which led to getting her heart broken. As she grew up, she put away her feelings and her vulnerability just as she put away her dolls. She hid her feelings away where occasionally she might take a peek, but never for long. They always went back into hiding, powerful reminders of a time long ago, never to return.

Rita married twice and both husbands left her. She has been abandoned all her life. Caring means devastation to her. For Rita, men and her relationships with men were the problem. The answer was simple: Never let yourself get close to a man again. But she didn't know what to do with the loneliness and the ugly song endlessly playing from that giant boom-box in her brain: "You got what you deserved because you never measured up."

Rita is now in another relationship. Once again it isn't smooth sailing. Her new male friend says, "I don't know what to do. When I call her a lot and things are going well, Rita gets terribly frightened and pushes me away. When I don't call, she gets mad as a wet hen and accuses me of abandoning her. What am I supposed to do?"

Rita is learning to understand her patterns and responses. As she does it's becoming clearer that staying away from men isn't her answer. Making her new friend into every man she ever had a relationship with won't work either. She realizes he is neither her father nor her ex-husbands. They may have abandoned her, but he hasn't. Not yet. But Rita may make things so difficult that he has no choice but to fulfill her own prophecy.

ELDEN AND JANICE

They have been married for twenty-seven years. And yet, although they've been married all those years and have six children, they complain of being total strangers.

Elden is a towering, bearded man with a giant

voice. But, contrary to all outward appearances, he's a pushover. "I can't stand heavy-duty emotions," he says. "Whenever there's high-grade emotion around, I just wilt. I can't help it, I just do. It all sounds like another religious campaign against sin, with me being the biggest sinner. I can't stand it. I never want to fight or get angry. I just want to get away."

Janice is thin, wears glasses, and has grey-streaked hair. She so desperately wants to love and be loved that it oozes from every pore. Her father abandoned her family when she was young, and she deeply resented his betrayal. Rage was Janice's reaction to this situation, rage that exploded outward. There was no stuffing of feelings for Janice. Whenever she experienced a feeling of abandonment creeping up on her, which was frequently, she became angry and attacked.

Over the years, Elden and Janice have spent thousands of dollars on marriage counseling, but it hasn't accomplished much. The same pattern kept repeating itself. Janice would feel abandoned and attack. Elden, in the face of this high-voltage emotion, would withdraw. Janice would then feel even more abandoned, which triggered more anger.

Elden, of course, would withdraw further. This cycle was active for twenty-seven years. Finally, they decided that the only way there could be a healthy relationship between them was for each of them to begin to deal with their destructive issues on an individual basis. Without taking this step they could have no future together.

Instead of blaming each other as the source of their problem, Elden and Janice began looking at their own personal issues. They each dug into their pasts to discover their patterns. Then they made some decisions. Elden decided it wasn't fair to run away from emotions, no matter what he'd learned in the past or how normal it felt. He decided he needed to learn to stand still and face the reality around him. Janice discovered she had, in fact, made Elden her father. She decided it wasn't fair to expect Elden to behave in the same manner as her father had. She became aware that she had polluted every close relationship in her life with her fear of abandonment and her expectations of betrayal. She decided that not only was that unfair to Elden, it wasn't fair to herself.

DARLA

Darla's lovely face is almost always clouded by worry lines. Her head often droops, reminding people of a recently spanked puppy. If she had it all to do over, she swears she'd leave men alone forever. Darla is very good at apologizing. It doesn't matter if it's her fault. It doesn't matter if she knows it's not her fault. It doesn't matter if there's anything to apologize for. She apologizes. Profusely! And she hates it.

Slowly, by reflecting on her past, Darla came to recognize an all-too-familiar pattern. She now calls it male dependency. More than anything in the world, Darla wanted to be daddy's little girl. She treated her father like a king, but she never got his approval.

"My original sin," Darla says, "is that I was born a girl." Not knowing differently, she decided there must be something wrong with her if she wasn't accepted in an appropriate way by her father.

Ever conscious of trying to please her father, Darla found herself in a series of relationships with men who were carbon copies of him. She kept recreating the same system again and again—the one she hated. Again, whatever approval and acceptance Darla received in these relationships came as a result of taking the blame, confessing her shortcomings, and apologizing.

Twenty years later, Darla is continuing to do the same thing. She is still falling into the same patterns she detested so much in the past.

WHO'S DRIVING

YOUR BUS?

There are three basic principles running through these stories that lead us to the same question: *Who's driving your bus?* These principles are:

- Then is always now.
- What we live with we learn. What we learn we practice. What we practice we become.
- Loyalty to neurotic values and patterns creates chaos.

THEN IS ALWAYS NOW

The main issue involved in making changes always seems to be boundaries—the boundaries between then and now. The problem is we're not living in the precious present; we're stuck in an emotional migraine from the past. One of the keys to change is learning how to discern what is now from what was then. We have to keep asking ourselves: "Who am I dealing with here and now? Am I dealing with the real person in front of me, or am I making this person a reflection of someone from my past? What rules and boundaries am I operating within now—

those I choose now, or the hated rules and perceptions of the past?"

What is your boundary between then and now? When Elden wilts, he's still in yesterday being victimized by the barrage of destructive messages he heard relatives expound in the guise of religious zeal. Janice is still being abandoned by her father day after day, time after time. The tragedy of the past abandonment is compounded endlessly by continuously dragging it through the present.

Change cannot get under way until we learn the difference between then and now. Until we decide where we wish to pitch our tent. True, it takes a great deal of effort and re-education to do this, but it's a vital skill to develop.

WHAT WE PRACTICE WE BECOME

What we live with we learn. What we learn we practice. What we practice we become.

We don't set out to make ourselves miserable. We're not insane. We're not evil. We're not self-haters who glory in our own unhappiness. But the fact is, until we begin trying to make ourselves aware of just who is driving the bus, we automatically act out the rules and patterns we learned over many years of practice. We're constantly reinforcing these rules and patterns and creating situations that continue to reinforce them. We may think there's no other way life can be.

Until we learn to embrace change, we obediently continue to act out the rules, and the consequences of our lives are a direct reflection of the rules we obey. The tragedy is, many of us spend the majority of our lives blindly obeying rules we hate and want to reject. We may not even be aware that the old rules are in control. We may fail to see the connection between past rules and present consequences.

Until Rita and Darla become consciously aware of the rules they live by and set about establishing new, healthier ones, there will be no change in their lives. We need to put our attention right there in the trenches with the rules. What do you believe? What are your basic assumptions about your self-worth, what you deserve, and what life has in store for you? Whatever you believe you will infallibly act out and make real in your life.

When all is said and done, the question remains, *Who is driving your bus?* It's always you, of course, but fixated where? At what age? Acting out and reacting to which disastrous past event or series of events? When Darla apologizes today, how old is she? When Rita becomes stuck in her push-pull agony of fearing too much intimacy yet becoming enraged at the betrayal of a male friend for not calling her, how old is she?

LOYALTY AND CHAOS

Loyalty to neurotic values and patterns creates chaos. This principle seems self-evident until we realize that many of the values and patterns that control our lives are buried in our subconscious. We are not aware of them! We do not consciously declare any great loyalty to beliefs like "Everyone else is smarter than me." "I will always come out the loser." "Everyone who loves me will leave me." "I must hide, for if they ever knew the truth about me I'd be alone forever."

To begin the process of change we must clearly understand these misconceptions and stage a powerful civil war against them—a war so powerful that we no longer allow them to dictate our destiny. It is an enormous task, but our present and future peace and happiness hang on the outcome.

UNTYING

THE KNOTS

Marvelous things happen in our lives as we gain insight. Once we begin to understand the nature of our inner knots, much of our fear and sense of powerlessness lifts like fog before the morning sun.

Why we act and think as we do can be traced to the patterns we were exposed to in childhood. Once we begin to identify this connection, we're on the road to understanding ourselves. With this new awareness we begin to feel more capable of change. From here we can begin taking responsibility for what we must do to solidify these changes in our lives.

Ultimately, we're working toward compassionate self-acceptance and healing. To further the process of understanding, we'll look at five basic states of being—or abiding senses—that hold us back. These abiding senses that are a blight to successful living are:

- Alienation.
- Shame and guilt.
- Fear of abandonment.

- Violence.
- Inability to play.

ALIENATION

People often speak of alienation as never feeling at home. We may talk about being among many friends, yet feeling alone. One person said, "I always feel as if I'm on the outside of a store window looking in. I always feel on the outside, always abandoned, like I never belong."

SHAME AND GUILT

We grew up with shame if we grew up sensing that everything was our fault, that risk always meant failure, that we were inadequate and incompetent. No matter how much or how well we did, we didn't count. We may have learned that we were flawed in our deepest core. We may say, "I was All State, and they never came to see me play." Or, "I was in every play the school ever put on. I was the *lead* for God's sake, but no one ever came to see me perform!" These and similar comments illustrate where shame comes from. It becomes what we are rooted in. That's why we feel so guilty for being inadequate, not good enough, no matter how much we achieve.

FEAR OF ABANDONMENT

We grow up with fear of abandonment if it has been our experience that commitments don't last, that people always leave, that when there is anger and conflict the door slams shut on the way out. We end up believing that there's no other way it can be.

VIOLENCE

Whether we are perpetrators or victims, violence is a learned response. People who are violent have almost always experienced violence in their past. Those of us who are victims of violence saw others in our families in victim roles. Whether we are victims or perpetrators, the patterns we learned became normal. Either violence became our usual response, or we expected beatings or other forms of abuse.

INABILITY TO PLAY

If life was always rush hour and we were stuck in the middle of the street trying to stay alive, we didn't learn to go out and play. The same holds true if everything was always extremely serious. For many of us, it was. Our great task in life was to survive—that's pretty serious.

* * *

Rita, Elden and Janice and all the rest of us are just acting out the patterns and habits we've learned. As we practiced, we developed this "sense of," and it hangs around us like smog in a big city. Coming to understand our old patterns is the gateway to change. It is the first step in accepting things as they are and not making of them something they're not. We are now what we've been practicing.

A Sense of Well-being

We've examined the states of being that hold us back. Now let's examine the difference between a "feeling" and a "sense," or state of being. Feelings are temporary. They come and go. Sometimes we may feel angry, sad, happy, or loving. We may go from feeling happy one day to feeling angry the next. These feelings can also be immensely powerful and seemingly leave us with little or no free will.

A sense, as I use it here, is a state of being that may vary in intensity from time to time, but it is never far from conscious recognition. Some people live in a sense of positive expectation. The sun almost always shines for them. If they lose five dollars they find consolation that whoever finds it will need it more. At times things may happen that make them feel sad, but because of the sense they generally maintain, the sun soon comes out and their anticipation returns.

Conversely, others live in a state of worry. If they buy a new car, they worry about the first scratch. If they win a million dollars, they worry about taxes. On vacation in Hawaii, they worry about all that nasty sun and skin cancer. Occasionally something so good may happen that it momentarily blocks their worry. They may even smile. But worry is never far behind. As soon as the good feeling recedes, even a little, their life settles into the normal, comfortable, predictable sea of worry. They live in a state of worry; it is their sense, their home. Their state of being is not coincidence.

The following traits, when present, give us a sense of well-being and security:

- Positive predictability.
- An experience of being valued and trusted.
- Nonviolent resolution of conflict.
- A sense that the world is a safe and beneficial place to live and play.

Each of these traits is learned and taught in countless ways. Yet, living with each trait creates a sense of something wonderful and safe. Let us examine each point more fully.

POSITIVE PREDICTABILITY

Positive predictability means that at certain times and in certain seasons of our lives we expect to meet positive situations and responses. These rewarding experiences happen predictably. In healthy environments, holidays are observed as joyful times. In healthy environments, holidays are predictably celebrated one year after the last one. Rites of passage and successes are acknowledged. A healthy environment allows for rules to be set. Consequences are fair, smiles are shared, and an ear is lent. In general, physical and emotional needs are lovingly met.

Obviously, no family is perfect, and all people occasionally make mistakes. And yet, these expressions of positive predictability occur often enough for us to count on them. They become the norm.

BEING VALUED AND TRUSTED

In healthy families all members of the family are important. Children learn that there is time and room for them, and home is a safe place. Children learn that they are valued through being affirmed. Children as well as adults are encouraged to experiment creatively and to experience the pleasures of accomplishment. When we learn that we are intrinsically unique and valuable, we also learn that making mistakes doesn't mean we *are* mistakes. We learn that while risk taking is desirable, failure is not a disaster.

Invariably, adults with a good self-image have the marvelous head start of knowing they were special to their parents. They learned that indeed they were "mommy and daddy's little girl or boy." They learned there was no law against crying or expressing feelings.

People live up to, or down to, the expectations they accept as demanded of them. Since there are no perfect families, nearly all adults recall situations in which they were treated unfairly as children. Nevertheless, in healthy families there is enough consistent support and encouragement to learn of one's value and competence. And this allows adults with a good self-image to act in a responsible, free, and trusted manner.

NONVIOLENT RESOLUTION OF CONFLICT

People in healthy families know that conflict does not mean an attack on their personal integrity. They know that even when things don't go right, an atmosphere of safety and nurturing is maintained. Anger is resolved through direct communication; rage is not appropriate. We learn to live with normal expressions of anger without fear of someone's getting mad.

Healthy children know the difference between anger and rage. They know that, even when angry, people don't hit others or hurl insults. They learn that conflict and not getting one's way doesn't mean slamming fists on the table or shouting and cursing. People in healthy families know that they are not automatically to blame for the disagreement. They do not become scapegoats, nor do they expect to be punished when there is conflict. People in healthy environments trust that anger won't hurt them. They also know that anger is not a tool for manipulating others.

THE WORLD AS A SAFE PLACE

Healthy people know how to play, because they trust that the world is safe. They know that there are times allotted for play—that there isn't always priority work to be done. They also know that play is not appropriate if there is major work that needs to be done. The middle of harvest is not the best occasion to take a week off and go to the islands. People who live in healthy environments know that the world tends to be a safe place, and that every minute of every day is not like walking through a mine field.

When we have these four basic "senses of," we develop the following characteristics:

- A sense of belonging in the world—a sense of home.
- A sense of adventure and willingness to achieve.
- A sense of trust—commitments and relationships are safe.
- A sense of nonviolence, of peace in the face of conflict.
- The ability to play and to celebrate life.

Again, when we have a sense of positive predictability, we also feel a sense of belonging. The experience of being valued and trusted gives us a sense of achievement. When commitments last, we gain a sense of trust. Nonviolent resolution of conflict helps us develop a sense that the world is a safe place to play.

THE TIES

THAT BIND

We've looked at our family patterns; now we're ready to consider the religious moral codes we grew up with, and society's impact on our lives. While neither of these forces in our lives is considered evil, they're not automatically healthy and to our benefit. In fact, the puritanical religious values that our country was founded on are often so entrenched in our societal expectations that it's very difficult to separate them from each other.

Moral Codes

For some of us, the moral codes that govern our lives can sometimes leave us feeling as though we can never measure up. In the following pages, we'll look at some of these qualities.

ALWAYS BE BUSY, ALWAYS PRODUCE

Many of us had the concept drilled into us that we are responsible for healing the world. We perhaps grew up in homes where we were made to feel responsible for everyone's behavior. If we took the blame for any miserable event, we probably bought the command of "Always keep working, for the salvation of the world depends on you."

While there is some merit in being responsible and making a difference in our world, we need to remember our boundaries, or perhaps establish them for the first time. Healthy boundaries translate into an approach to life that sounds more like this: "I can make a difference in my world, not *everyone's* world." This basic truth may fly in the face of our egos, but change starts with ourselves, not with others.

If we grew up with the sense that it was our task to save the world, that it was our moral imperative to keep producing at all costs, chances are we also learned that leisure is definitely not desirable. It might even be sinful. "How can I relax when there's so much to do and all of it is my responsibility?"

Thus, the basic message, "Thou shalt not play," was learned. Now, as adults, we act out patterns devoid of play, with the understanding that this is virtuous! We have come to believe that we are more worthy when we are hard at work, or at least being busy, than when we are relaxing, having fun.

PENANCE AND REJECTING PLEASURE

Many of us learned from our religious moral codes that, more than anything else, we are sinners. We were conceived in sin, born in sin, and live in sin. Given this, it's a short step from believing we're inferior to believing we're probably beyond redemption. Sinfulness fits us like a custom-made suit of clothes because it agrees with our learned self-image.

It's a matter of boundaries. While we may be inadequate in some ways, these qualities do not make up our whole being. We are also wonderful, loving, beloved, and necessary human beings. We are born with a hunger for love and a thirst for the good. These qualities are inherent within us.

If we buy the message of right and wrong, however, we buy into the concept that we need to be punished. If we already believe that a life of hurt and pain is our destiny, we may accept the message of penance from a shame-based moral code. When this sense is further compounded with messages of inadequacy from our families, we carry an unbearable load.

If sacrifice and hurting are of high moral value,

pleasure is not. Pleasure of any kind, including sexual expression or enjoying financial success, must be rejected. Many of us who no longer observe religious traditions are still bent down by these moral commands. Acts of pleasure may leave us feeling guilty, shamed, and undeserving. If we feel undeserving, we may think we deserve to be punished. We may even create our own punishment by acts that could include ruining a potentially successful relationship or entering an abusive relationship.

SELF-DENIAL

Self-denial means doing without whatever we want or desire. The more we want or desire an object or activity, the more merit there is to the self-denial. We adopt various reasons for doing without. We tell ourselves it's because it builds character, because God wants it. The net result is that a great deal of good that could have entered our lives doesn't. A big part of change is allowing ourselves to enjoy the good in life.

If we hold self-denial in high regard, it's very likely that we don't often treat ourselves to pleasurable experiences because this would be of low moral value. Treating ourselves means willingly taking time off for fun and play; taking vacations; lying around the house doing nothing—and liking it. Treating ourselves means allowing ourselves to get into win-win situations in both our career and relationships. It means allowing ourselves to love and be loved, to join healthy communities, and even to take a bubble bath. Treating ourselves may be ordering the meal we really like in a restaurant, starting a stamp collection, or getting a massage. Treating ourselves is noticing the beauty of nature, enjoying the fun of a wedding celebration, or delighting in a child's wonder.

BLIND OBEDIENCE

We may have been raised with the belief that there was no religious moral command higher than blind obedience. Those of us who did as we were told without questioning were often praised. And when messages and orders came from authority figures, these were tough waters to swim against. It didn't matter whether the ideas made sense to us. It was immaterial whether our own values were compromised by what we were told to do. It was simply expected that we would follow the rules. And if we did follow the rules properly—dictated through a shame-based moral code—God would love us and we would go to heaven.

SOCIETAL

TRAPS

In an attempt to condense the list of societal traps that ensnare men and women today, I arrived at four demanding, powerful tenets that deepen and reinforce the whims of the ego and get in the way of the process of positive change.

- Always need what you don't have.
- Winning is a must.
- Relationships are a test of power.
- All gratification must be instant.

ALWAYS NEED WHAT YOU DON'T HAVE

Much of our western economy is based on the selling of goods and services. This selling is based on creating real or imagined needs. Advertising is perpetually directing messages at us that imply we're inadequate unless we drive a luxury car or dress a certain way. The reverse side of this message is, "If you do have our product you will belong and have the status you desire." While advertising serves a valid role in our economy, we need to be aware of how vulnerable we are to such messages.

Implied messages, such as "You will be loved and accepted if you use our product," are compelling. Many of us are all but helpless when we hear the siren call of Madison Avenue promising love and acceptance.

I've often heard it said, "If you are enough, you will always have enough. But if you aren't enough, nothing will be enough." The whole issue with fear that often drives our egos is that we think we aren't enough.

WINNING IS A MUST

The point of competition, the way we practice it in our society, is to see who wins, who's the best. We have a passion to be number one. No one remembers who came in second. And yet, many of us abhor competition because it's often a reminder that we aren't up to the mark. We failed again.

However, some of us hear the familiar self-defeating messages and rebel. Determined not to be passive victims, we show everyone we aren't failures. We become defiant. We can never let ourselves lose. We compulsively recount our exploits, our latest victory, our successes.

But who is "everyone"? Who are we directing all this energy and effort toward? Who is it we're trying to prove our worth to?

Who? All the people in our past who are alive in us today, whose messages are still being picked up on our antennae. Whether we're overbearing, compulsive achievers or passive, victimized people pleasers, we're reacting to the messages of the past. Many of us, in our own way, are allowing an angry, sad child to drive our bus.

The early Greeks viewed competition simply as competition with the self. Although the winner received the laurel wreath, the idea of competition was to expand one's limits, to better one's personal best. The Greek word for excellence, *arete*, indicated a person who was in balance. The idea was to pursue excellence in all areas of life—physical, spiritual, and intellectual. Being the best runner mattered little if that runner wasn't also well versed in other important areas of life. Few of us today have such a sane, balanced sense of competition. Our society teaches us that competition is always against others, and the outcome determines who is best.

Life may indeed be a race, but what freedom to

be running in the right competition, striving to be balanced individuals at peace with ourselves.

RELATIONSHIPS ARE A TEST OF POWER

Much of our society's focus on relationships concerns who gets who. Having sex with someone is considered a "score." The whole issue is centered around who wins and who loses. Who will be the boss, and who will do as they are told. While attitudes about male and female roles have changed over the past few decades, power struggles in relationships are still widespread. The core of the issue is still: "If you give in, you lose."

The hero of many of our adventure stories is still the solitary, unknown, mystery man who never really fits into the community mold, but wanders along the fringes of society doing what no one else can do. When the task is over and heroic feats have been accomplished, the loner invariably drifts off to another supposed adventure. Before he drifts off, he usually has a sexual encounter with the most desirable woman available. She is often totally helpless in the face of the uncommitted hero.

These stories teach us that commitments don't

last and the person with the power is the one who does not or cannot nurture, or communicate, or commit. Once again, we may be bombarded with the same messages that relationships are tests of power—and we have none. Therefore, since we have no power, the only sane thing to do is take what we can get. Without their realizing it, the character of many men is formed in the school that teaches the real "men of action" are the drifters, that real excitement only comes to those who hit and run, and that an expression of commitment and living responsibility is boring.

ALL GRATIFICATION MUST BE INSTANT

It's no secret that we live in an age of instant gratification. Everything, from coffee to potatoes to love, must be instant. Worth is all too often determined by speed. We burn ourselves out trying to do everything fast—and right. But since we can't do anything "right enough," no matter how much or how well we achieve, we still feel inferior about our performance. This insanity of instant gratification becomes a giant obstacle to meaningful change and growth.

We may believe, unrealistically, that satisfaction should be instant or at least quicker than it is. When it isn't immediate, all the old messages like *There must be something wrong with me . . . I haven't done it right . . . I can probably never do it right . . .* vault into place. These old messages rush to the front of the bus, shove reason out of the driver's seat, and speed off on the familiar road of devastation.

Getting ourselves off the bus requires taking stock of where we're headed. We didn't suddenly get stuck on this route, and we won't get instantly unstuck. "Every lovely thing takes time to grow." When we demand instant results and gratification, we sacrifice the true rewards of life, the ones that can only be gained through patience and consistent efforts aimed at healthy growth. When we don't give ourselves the time we need for the process of change, we pay a heavy price—we deepen the old ego-driven habits that enslave us.

I'll Do It to Me Again

As people on the dynamic road of change, we've looked at destructive messages from society and its moral codes, and we've looked at how our families have influenced and affected us. The final concept that holds us back is our tendency to create situations that perpetuate the same painful consequences we so want to escape. I have heard this described as the "I'll do it to me again" syndrome.

We often say, "Why does this keep happening to me?" as though it's all bad luck. Somehow, we repeatedly "catch" disaster like catching the flu from viruses we're defenseless against.

Change begins when we realize we're stuck in self-defeating cycles. Luck or unseen forces have nothing to do with it. Change begins when we realize that we're acting out patterns and creating situations as a result of the painful consequences of our own behavior. As adults, we're the ones who all too often create the situations we detest.

Suzanne told of how she didn't make enough money to live on. She was sick and tired of people's problems, and of never having the time or money for a vacation. How did she create this situation? She was a county crisis-intervention worker, and focused on the worst problems human beings are capable of having. She worked for near minimum wage and did not get paid for the countless hours of overtime she put in. And yet, no matter what anyone suggested about how she might free herself from this self-defeating cycle, Suzanne had a reason why it was impossible to change.

THE PROGRESSION

OF CHANGE

The journey of change moves us from stress to integrity. Its momentum depends on two things:

- Understanding the principle of using our heads, not our hearts, to identify well-worn, destructive patterns.
- Understanding the relationship between these old patterns and today's pain.

Using Our Heads, Not Our Hearts

Our hearts—our actual feelings—have been in control for a long time. That control now fits like a custom-made suit of clothes. But if we continue being directed solely by our feelings, we can experience nothing new.

All patterns as well as their consequences become normal with practice, and all behavior, practiced enough, becomes habit. Our current habits seem normal to us now, and they will fight to the death to survive. But if what we have learned, practiced, become, and accepted as normal are neurotic and self-limiting behaviors, we must be willing to go to war with what we've come to think of as "normal."

At the beginning of this process of change we don't recognize the power of habits. For this reason, it will be necessary to frequently reassess goals and behaviors to determine whether we're still on target. The tendency is to reason, "If I understand it, I should be master of it." Then our old familiar habits of thought kick in to add, "and master of it *now!*"

What we initially think is enormous insight is often only a weak glimpse at best. It may take months, even years, before we truly see ourselves with clarity. And even if we do see a pattern clearly, it doesn't necessarily mean that anything has changed. Old patterns cannot be torn out and overthrown without a major fight waged on several fronts.

Old Patterns and Present Pain

Our feelings are one of the primary fronts we have to face in order to change. Old patterns often fight back with physical symptoms. When confronting an old pattern—perhaps by standing up for ourselves and asking for what we need—we may feel panicked, tired, depressed, or confused. A side effect of our feelings may be a physical reaction. While in the grip of those feelings, our knees may shake, our stomachs may roll, our necks may tighten up, and our hands may sweat.

Another defense is to hide our feelings behind rationalizations. On top of feeling panicky and shaky, we may conjure up compelling reasons to avoid following through with the actions required to create change in our lives. For example, in a relationship when something needs to be said, we may tell ourselves, *They don't really care,* followed quickly with, *and I don't care either.* Or, *Tomorrow is a better time.* Another example may be, *Why should I have to be the one to bring this up? It's not fair. I won't say anything till they do or I will lose my integrity.*

Peace at any price can slide into the driver's seat with such thoughts as: *It really is a favor to them not to bring this up. It may hurt their feelings. Since I'm basically a nice person, I will, in the name of goodness, be doing the virtuous thing by keeping my mouth shut.* We can expect to encounter what seems like perfectly logical reasoning when we attempt change. Such thoughts and feelings are just our old habits protecting themselves.

DESTRUCTIVE DELAYING TACTICS

Another stumbling block to change is medicating our discomfort with more destructive, compulsive behavior. For example, rather than dealing directly with a time-rooted habit, some of us will go on a spending binge, while others of us delay buying things we desperately need. Some of us bury ourselves in our jobs or other forms of busyness, like excessive volunteer work when time for ourselves is already scarce. Some of us will do anything rather than stand still and face a newly dawning reality.

When our feelings are leading us, we may find ourselves looking for excuses to look up an old lover. Perhaps we're presently involved in a relationship requiring new behavior and we're not feeling up to the challenge. The truth may be that we find it difficult to remain committed to one person. Rather than examining this tendency to shy away from commitment, we may return to our old patterns. When our hearts pull us back toward unhealthy relationships of the past, we need to consider the consequences of such behavior. We need to let our heads recognize the potential danger of such a pull. If we truly desire change and serenity—the ultimate stress relief—we need to be willing, for a while, to be led by our heads.

Stress Relief

An effective program of change gradually accomplishes three things. It:

- Relieves stress.
- Enables us to reclaim our power and integrity.
- Generates hope.

Repeating unhealthy habits is extremely stressful. Yet the stress, like the cycle that creates it, becomes so normal and we grow so used to it that the stress goes almost unnoticed. Our attitude becomes, *Doesn't everyone live like this?* A few much too commonly accepted symptoms of the stress many of us learn to live with are:

- Chronic fatigue.
- Fitful sleep.
- Digestive problems.
- Impatience and irritability.
- Emotional withdrawal.

Annette never thought of herself as stressed. She just never got a good night's sleep. At times her pulse raced, and she frequently had headaches. If she was asked how she was doing, Annette would smile sweetly and say, "I'm fine. Thanks for asking," even when these signs of stress were present.

Stress symptoms don't just happen. They're caused by behavior that is destructive, even though it might feel normal. For example, let's look at one week in Sam's life as he faces mounting stress. Despite the confusion and pain he felt from so many different fronts of his life, Sam had no inkling that he was living under enormous stress.

The woman Sam had been having an extramarital affair with dumped him, but he was glad because he didn't really like her. Earlier, he hadn't been able to figure out how to tell her this, so he introduced her to his best friend, hoping they'd hit it off. They did, but Sam felt guilty because he knew this girl was only after someone to take care of her.

On top of this, in the same week, Sam's wife decided she didn't want to work on their relationship anymore. Then his car had to go back to the shop to be fixed three times. And to top it all off he seriously considered quitting his safe and lucrative job to take a once-in-a-lifetime stab at a get-rich-quick scheme.

Just look at all the issues that have created absolute chaos in Sam's life. First of all, Sam has to learn to live honestly no matter how he thinks others may regard him. If he chooses to remain married, having an affair hopelessly complicates his life. Rather than palming his lover off on his best friend, Sam needed to listen to his head and tell the woman that the relationship was over.

Sam must learn that feelings alone can't dictate his behavior. Feeling guilty and powerless is a way of life for Sam—he often feels he has done something wrong. But if he decides to deal with his day-to-day problems with integrity, Sam can learn he has no need to feel guilty. Looking at his past can show him where these lessons came from and how acting out old patterns can keep his life in chaos.

As it turned out, Sam opened up to new insights and slowly turned those insights into solid change. He learned to make better decisions and act on them.

Reclaiming Integrity

Loss of integrity causes stress. Many of us continue to sacrifice integrity for the sake of acceptance or escape. Loss of integrity results from behaving in a way that compromises our values. Granted, many of us have incorporated some neurotic values into our lives, but we also espouse many healthy values that we often violate. When we do this, we compromise our integrity. Instinctively, we respect certain values. But when our actions conflict with these values, we feel uneasy with ourselves, and these feelings fuel stress in our lives.

Some of the clearly unhealthy values in our lives might be perfectionism, passivism, and workaholism. These in turn may interfere with the basic healthy values we want to live by.

A few examples of these positive personal values that we undermine could be:

- Honesty.
- Freedom from abuse.
- Confidence to do the best we can.

Some of the stressful societal values we've learned might include:

- Getting a just reward for work done.
- Being a success by getting ahead.
- Looking "right."

HONESTY

Most of us don't so much lie as make alibis, blame, and adopt delusion and denial as a way of life. We may practice dishonesty when we accept a person or statement we know is not true. We may be dishonest when we associate with people we really don't like but are afraid to leave.

Many of us desperately need the love and acceptance we never got as children and are still trying to find many years later. This need leaves us vulnerable to toxic, dependent relationships. Even though we may know such relationships don't work, we remain hooked. We keep telling ourselves, *Surely it will work this time.*

While no one is perfectly honest, these are the reasons many of us tend to be dishonest with ourselves and others. Every time we're dishonest with ourselves, a bit of integrity slips away and with it self-esteem. Ultimately, the result is stress.

FREEDOM FROM ABUSE

In a society that espouses and sponsors freedom from abuse, it is ironic that many of us live with abuse in one or more areas of our lives. The most common example involves those of us who live within unhealthy families. As children we may have had no choice. And yet, as adults, we marry people who abuse us. Or perhaps we marry a wonderful person, but become frightened and ruin the relationship. Even more difficult to understand are women who repeatedly call old boyfriends who abused them. Or men who continue to call former girlfriends who have rejected or manipulated them.

This form of self-abuse may be the result of "euphoric recall." When we're feeling alone, abandoned, or betrayed—when the eight-year-old is in the driver's seat—we may recall the old days with a sense of fondness. We forget all the torment and the pain, and convince ourselves that it was all much better than it really was. We become so convinced by our wishful thinking that we try to go back to the old situation again, even though we sense it's a mistake. When we do this, our integrity diminishes and stress skyrockets.

Some of us tolerate abuse at the workplace. The working world is not exempt from unhealthy situations—many jobs are unduly pressure packed and deadline oriented. This situation, too, may be difficult to escape if we've become accustomed to a higher wage. Or, at the other end of the spectrum, we may lack the education to find a better job.

In any of these situations, we must remember that, at first, when we're trying to break old patterns, making changes may seem more stressful. But delaying change simply keeps the stress ongoing. Once a pattern begins to crumble, stress decreases each time we reinforce our new behavior and thought processes. Before long, the changes we're making begin to feel much more comfortable than our old way of doing things.

DOING THE BEST WE CAN

As children most of us were taught that we are to do the best we can, exercise our potential, and make of ourselves everything we possibly can. But these phrases, heard from our parents and commencement speakers, and indeed all of society, often contain double messages. On the one hand, we may be taught these values, while on the other hand we may be told that we are dumb, incompetent, and lucky just to be alive. While the basic message of "go for it" is part of our heritage, many of us may find ourselves underemployed, underpaid, undereducated, under everything. Many of our lives are living contradictions to the message of "do your best."

We often limit ourselves from living up to our potential in specific areas. If we are tremendous cooks, we may not enter our work in the county fair to try for a blue ribbon. We may justify it with something like "It just isn't my cup of tea," or "I could never win." This denies the value of doing our best when the truth may be "I'd love to enter this contest, win, and wear the blue ribbon on my chest for one whole year! And, I'd like to do that just to spite all those people who told me I was second best."

The negative image we have of ourselves often doesn't allow us to embrace our birthright. And yet, we really want to do our best. When we don't, integrity suffers—whether it is cooking, being the best salesperson in the company, or allowing ourselves to enjoy our lives and relax.

GETTING A JUST REWARD

Many of us feel unacknowledged, unappreciated, even unseen. Women often speak of feeling hurt because their opinions are never asked, their special efforts are never recognized, and their love is taken for granted. They may see their mates ignoring them, yet displaying concern and tenderness toward others, and volunteering time to help neighbors, friends, or even casual acquaintances. These women are not getting their just reward for work done because they get none of the "good stuff."

Men, too, more often than anyone imagines, have this value violated. Men also tend to be people pleasers, sacrificing integrity. Many men feel that they are just a paycheck and provider. They feel uncared for and taken for granted.

Not being rewarded for our accomplishments becomes a cycle, feeding our insecurities and low self-esteem. To break this cycle and restore our integrity, we may have to leave unhealthy relationships or find better jobs. A less drastic action, but one just as frightening, involves speaking up for our rights. While these may seem like very stressful actions, they are actually the beginning of eliminating stress-laden patterns.

GETTING AHEAD

Our culture strongly emphasizes the importance of moving always upward. Success, to most of us, means getting ahead, moving up in the world. Even if we don't consciously embrace this value, we're surrounded by it. Those of us who aren't forging forward obviously don't have the "right stuff." We are flawed, a judgment that sounds familiar enough to most of us. When we accept this value, many of us slam headfirst into the brick wall of shame. On the one hand there's the imperative to move ahead. On the other, there's the shaming self-criticism, "Sure, but I really can't. I can't do anything right."

Some of us are overachievers. We obsessively and compulsively achieve materially, but the success we win at a great price brings us little joy. The success is never enough. Why? It may be that we're still trying to please someone from our past who we were never able to satisfy.

The great price we pay for our material success is

sometimes an inability to have healthy, nurturing relationships. We have no time because we're driving ourselves to achieve. Beyond that we often tend to treat relationships in the same manner as business projects. We often manipulate, look for the angles, and refuse to be at risk. Relationships cannot live in such an environment.

Then, there are some of us who are passive and hate to make decisions. Our indecisiveness may drive our mates insane. This may occur in situations such as dealing with children from a previous marriage. As hard and impervious as we might be in business, we become victims in the face of personal relationships. We allow ourselves to be used shamefully. We may refuse to see through the most obvious games of those to whom we are vulnerable. We are often overwhelmed with feelings of guilt. The bottom line is that our sense of self-worth is being destroyed. There is a conflict between our values and our behavior.

LOOKING "RIGHT"

It's difficult to pinpoint just what "right" means here. It keeps changing. Basically, the "right" look is what many of us see ourselves as not having. Advertisements are constantly telling us that if we dress correctly, or use the right toothpaste, or drive the right car, we will magically get all the approval we never had. The power of this promise is proportionate to the deprivation each of us has suffered.

This list of six values is certainly not definitive. These values may not even be in your top ten. But by understanding the dynamic of values clashing with behaviors, you gain a clear insight about where your personal sense of integrity comes from and how it gets stripped away. It's in that loss of integrity that we experience stress.

LIVING A LIFE

OF FREEDOM

It has been said, "Everyone wants to go to heaven but no one wants to die." Most of us can relate to that. Going to heaven is a good analogy for change with its implied sense of freedom, of finally breaking habits learned so long ago and practiced ever since.

Change is often difficult. We may have to make heroic decisions that fly in the face of our old habits. But no matter how difficult it may seem, we can break the chains. Freedom can be won.

Now, those are fine words. Ones we'd expect to find in a book such as this. But they come from deep personal experience. I know the power of those old habits, the incredible power they have to bind, blind, and fool us into believing there really is no other way to live. I know how impossible it may seem to have anything other than frustrating relationships. I know how hard it is to declare our feelings and demand our rights. Just the suggestion can seem like a cruel joke. To many of us, the ability to relax, play, and enjoy life can seem remote—something other people do while we sit on the sidelines.

But I have also experienced the other side of this

coin. And I know many people who have been able to open their lives to freedom, to hope, and change.

Hope

A true sense of hope is essential to every process of change. Hope is the voice that tells us life will improve, that our self-defeating cycle is not permanent. But hope eventually demands proof to be legitimate. The proof hope demands is successful behavior. As we make concrete, real life strides in breaking old habits, we will experience heartening results. Those results grow into a body of evidence that the habits can be broken.

- Rita needs to realize that she deserves the good stuff, the love and respect everyone deserves. When she gains self-love, she will have hope.
- Darla must realize that she can be an independent person, and her self-esteem does not have to be based on approval from men or others. When she discovers this freedom, she will feel hope.

Change

Our proof need not be total nor once and for all. Change doesn't happen like that. We didn't learn how to be who we are all at once, and we don't unlearn it immediately. However, once we start behaving differently, we discover a new source of hope—ourselves.

The behaviors that create an effective change and generate hope are those that contradict old patterns. If we are reclusive, speaking our feelings and thoughts is what is needed. If we lack esteem for ourselves, tooting our own horn until we believe ourselves is our need. If we practice the principle "It's my way or the highway," then we need to ease up, listen, and hear other people's needs as well.

While we can probably find a hundred different ways to put destructive habits behind us, all successful change must include the following steps.

- Desire it.
- Choose it.
- Act it.
- Keep on keeping on.

These items may seem obvious in their simplicity, but they require dedication to carry out.

DESIRE IT

Since fierce habits guard the path of change, we must desire to confront them more than we fear not to. To illustrate this point, it may be helpful to you to write two paragraphs as an activity:

- In the first paragraph, outline the benefits of change. What can you gain if you go to war with your habits? What will it mean to you? How important is it?
- In the second paragraph write down what you could lose if you choose not to change. What have you chosen for yourself? How badly do the chains of the old cycle hurt? What price are you paying for not making the effort to change?

These two paragraphs probably won't change your life. But they will offer clarification about the quality of life you have chosen.

CHOOSE IT

Wishes are not decisions. Change demands that we make a genuine decision, one from which we do not retreat. In order to do this we need to take a look at some elements of effective decision making:

- **If nothing changes, nothing changes.** Many of us end up doing exactly the same things in a different way. The changes we make must produce different results in our lives.
- **Do we need to make a decision?** If we're suffering in an ongoing situation, it's likely that a decision to change is needed.
- **Identify and clarify the issues.** Very often, the issue as we see it turns out to not be the issue at all. We must examine the situation carefully and determine whether a decision will positively affect our intentions.
- **There is no hell in the world like indecision.** Indecision means we continue with our life as it is, in emotional paralysis and pain. What price are we willing to pay for not making a decision?
- **It's possible to accumulate evidence forever.** Accumulating evidence is a necessary step in decision making, but we must not delude our-

selves by spending the rest of our lives doing it. There is no easy way out of making large decisions, and no way to make everyone happy.

- **It's possible to decide and then not act.** Once we make decisions, we are in a different place spiritually and emotionally. If we don't act on our decision, we are apt to become miserable, angry, and depressed because we've lied to ourselves.
- **Once we make a decision and act on it, we often find it's a two-foot jump, rather than a two-mile jump.** When looking at our painful decisions in retrospect, we wonder why we waited so long.
- **It's possible to wait so long we lose the ability to decide.** We must be honest with ourselves regarding this point. If we need to make a decision but postpone the necessary action, we may reach a point where we're no longer able to choose. Then we may be stuck with the situation for the rest of our lives.
- **When we're ready to make a decision, we will make it, and not before.** Making decisions about our deep, primary habits and patterns involves more than rational choice. It

involves an inner, spiritual determination. The decision to change is often a conversion experience.

- **It's normal to feel grief and pain at the moment we make a decision.** Something else must end in order for something new to begin. Often a heavy decision calls for closure. We need to remember that grief and pain are natural, but they don't last forever.
- **Once we have made our decision, never look back.** It's tragic to spend the rest of our lives thinking about what we lost. We must focus on what we have gained.
- **We cannot do it alone.** We all need emotional support when we make difficult decisions. It's important to find a person with whom we can share our decisions. Sharing with a healthy friend helps us remain faithful to our decision. It also helps prevent us from stepping backward into the same situation.

ACT IT

While desire and decision are necessary to recovery, they only prepare us. The real work of change is altering our behavior. Insight is important, but insight is not change. Change demands different behavior. We build our integrity by proving to ourselves that we have options. The successes we achieve provide proof that builds hope and grants rewards. The rewards offer the sense of our own worth, the thrill of discovering that our decisions can have positive consequences. We were affected by our pasts, but we need not be victims.

Once we have decided to change, we need to follow some basic guidelines and perform some simple activities with each.

- Do what counts.
- Avoid lose/lose situations.
- Decide on a major blow for freedom.
- Keep on keeping on.

DO WHAT COUNTS

Motion without direction is ineffective. Our behavior ultimately contradicts our old neurotic patterns. The more we behave with the conscious intent of breaking old patterns, the more effective our action. Getting a haircut may just be a routine task. However, we could approach it with the attitude that *I am getting my hair cut for the specific reason that I deserve to look my best.* This gives our decision to get a haircut a whole new level of power, especially if we get a new style or spend more than usual.

While this may seem a minor thing, be aware that we must celebrate even the smallest gain. It may take many baby steps before we're ready to make a giant step. Be patient. Build the yellow brick road one brick at a time.

Activity: Decide on one pattern you feel ready to break. Next, determine the specific, daily behavior you're willing to undertake for that end.

AVOID LOSE/LOSE SITUATIONS

All the positives in the world will do us little good if we don't refrain from behaviors that enforce unhealthy habits. As we daily lay another brick in our new road, we must be aware of letting go of old behavior that robs us of our newfound integrity. New behaviors—such as exercising regularly, applying for a new job, or going back to school—must prove to us that we count. But we have to remember that all our new behaviors could be cancelled by one old pattern, such as continuing to date an abusive person.

Again, we do it one baby step at a time. For a while we may not be able to make the big jumps—such as ending a toxic relationship—but we must be aware that such a jump will be called for eventually. When the time comes for such a jump, we will be ready—made ready by all the step-by-step progress done on a daily basis.

Activity: Just as you listed behaviors that hold you to the old patterns, now list the situations that will keep you from winning, from breaking the patterns.

DECIDE ON A MAJOR BLOW FOR FREEDOM

Deciding to do a primary project, often considered for years, creates a major jump on the integrity scale. Such a major jump may be:

- Getting in shape and eating nutritiously.
- Getting a totally new hair fashion.
- Going on a vacation.
- Making a phone call you have been putting off for months or years.
- Finally asking *that* person for a date.
- Starting a savings account.

Powerful possibilities like these vary as much as individuals. Even though such one time actions are not permanent, they provide a good place to start. Such behaviors give us a boost. To achieve real freedom, however, we must continue to build and move forward—we must keep on keeping on if we want to make progress.

Keep on Keeping On

While we can expect old habits to resist change, our new commitment to growth generates such energy and enthusiasm that we are apt to take off like a rocket. The challenge is to keep the rocket in orbit. That takes support. Change not surrounded by a support system will not last.

Activity: Building your support system is your next endeavor.

Part of the task of creating a support system is to stick with winners. While we do need the company of others, we need to avoid losers. Instead, we need those who provide support by the quality of their lives, by their caring comments, by the interests they have, and by the way they live such interests.

Often, we may not be aware of the difference this makes, but we are changing. We hear fewer negative comments like "I can't . . ." "Life is so unfair . . ." We more frequently hear, "This is what I am doing . . ." "Isn't this exciting . . ." "It felt so good . . ." "My plan for tomorrow is . . ."

Each of us reflects our community. Many of us don't even suspect there could be other ways of thinking, feeling, and acting. There are other ways. Our blind spots may prevent us from seeing them or even seeking them out, but they are there. We can become one of the winners.

Spirituality

Spirituality is a critical element of living a more peaceful life. Many people find prayer and meditation essential. Many find that without conscious contact with a Higher Power, the journey is made much more difficult. Many will tell you the journey is not possible at all without such assistance.

Faith is a personal reality. One's concept of God is uniquely individualistic. And while our concepts of God may have been influenced and manipulated by events of our past, many of us now realize our need for God's help. We arrive at a unique understanding of God. As we grow, we find a deeper ability to relate to a God who is loving, who is powerful on our behalf, and who, most importantly, cares about us. As with the rest of change, such realization may come slowly and at a cost. This is the way anything of value comes to us. But it's worth the effort. It's a necessary part of change and growth.

We Can Because We Think We Can

Some things I cannot change: my age, who my relatives are, my eye color, my height, my childhood experiences, my inborn talents, my nature, whether the sun will shine, my job history, what I will inherit, how my parents feel, yesterday's lost opportunities, how long I will live, who forgives me, how my parents treated me, how much I am loved, the past.

Some things I can change: the youthfulness of my spirit, who my friends are, my adult experiences, my achievements, my character, whether my eyes will shine, my job possibilities, what I will bequeath, how I feel, my ability to act on today's opportunities, how well I will live, whom I forgive, how I treat my own children, how much I love, the future.

These concluding pages are about confidence—that elusive, yet essential quality of success. I'm not talking about success or confidence in general, but rather success in our journey of change, our confidence that the journey can be achieved.

As hard as it may be for many of us to allow ourselves a feeling of confidence, the results can be remarkable. Confidence creates a feeling of awe, a soaring of the mind, a mightiness of spirit, a largeness of soul. All together, these form an underlying sense of accomplishment that generates success. Not much can happen without confidence.

Henry Ford is credited with having said, "Whether you think you can or think you can't—you're right." Confidence is like that. As the Roman poet Virgil said in his inspired words from the *Aeneid:* "They can because they think they can."

These words are as true for us today as they were for the people of ancient Rome. If we think we can succeed, or come to think we can, we will. If not, no matter how much theory we have, no matter how clear the exercises may be, no matter how good our intentions, nothing much will change.

It's true that we've been practicing to be who we are for a very long time—all our lives in fact. We may have learned to be experts at some patterns of behavior and thoughts that are self-defeating and self-destructive. We may have learned to skillfully practice denial, rather than face reality. We may have learned to practice fear rather than courage; self-delusion rather than honesty; perfectionism rather than the acceptance of ourselves as imperfect people in an imperfect world; resentment rather than forgiveness.

Certainly this is true. But what else is true is that it need not remain so! Whether it does is a question of self-confidence.

Note the difference between the biblical accounts of Moses and David. Moses was given the great task of leading his people through the desert and into the promised land. He didn't think he could. He thought he was too weak, the task too big, the enemy too strong. But in time, he came to learn he was up to the task.

Little David, on the other hand, knew from the first moment that the giant Goliath would fall before him. Apparently, confidence was not a problem for him as it was for Moses and most of the rest of us.

Moses came to believe; he slowly gained the confidence that he could lead his people to freedom. David knew it from the start. In both cases, confidence and faith made achievement possible. Confidence can allow us to plug into our Higher Power. Confidence helps us feel we are not alone, that the task can be done, that all the power necessary to change is at hand. Confidence holds high the torch when the chilling wind blows down the dark corridors of our minds telling us, "Get real! Who do you think you're kidding! The wounds are too deep, the hurt too permanent. You are who you are. You'll never be anything more!"

Only confidence can answer that challenge. Only confidence shouts back into the darkness, "That's right. I am who I am. And that means I'm a person who, with the support of others and with the grace of my Higher Power, can go where I will. I can do, and be what I choose. And I choose freedom!"

Confidence is gained by the repeated experience of success. The early steps we take on that personal road of success may seem trivial. Initially we share a feeling—perhaps saying "No" for the first time.

Then we ask for what we need, perhaps voicing our own opinions for the first time. These expressions might be directed at the family dog, but at least we've said them to something alive!

Sometimes what gets us going is a positive comment from a friend or co-worker. Or we may notice the look on a loved one's face that has been there for years—and realize the problem this time. Perhaps the stories of fellow pilgrims who have fought the same battles we have can inspire us. We hear them and say to ourselves, "If they can do it, so can I." Or at least we begin to think we can. And so the journey begins again with new power.

ABOUT THE AUTHORS

Earnie Larsen and Carol Larsen Hegarty have co-authored two daily meditation books, *Days of Healing, Days of Joy* and *Believing in Myself.* The author of numerous self-help and inspirational books, including *Stage II Recovery,* Earnie Larsen is known to a large national audience for his PBS program, "Believing in Yourself."